QUICK, LET'S GET OUT OF HERE

MICHAEL ROSEN
AND QUENTIN BLAKE

PUFFIN POETRY

PUFFIN BOOKS

UK | USA | Canada | Ireland | Australia
India | New Zealand | South Africa

Puffin Books is part of the Penguin Random House group of companies
whose addresses can be found at global.penguinrandomhouse.com.

puffinbooks.com

First published by Andre Deutsch Ltd 1983
Published in Puffin Books 1985
Reissued in this edition 2015
001

Text copyright © Michael Rosen, 1983
Illustrations copyright © Quentin Blake, 1983
All rights reserved

The moral right of the author and illustrator has been asserted

Set in Baskerville MT
Printed in Great Britain by Clays Ltd, St Ives plc

A CIP catalogue record for this book is available from the British Library

ISBN: 978-0-141-36297-7

www.greenpenguin.co.uk

PUFFIN POETRY

QUICK, LET'S GET OUT OF HERE

MICHAEL ROSEN was brought up in London. He originally tried to study medicine before starting to write poems and stories. His poems are about all kinds of things – but always important things – from chocolate cake to bathtime. He was Children's Laureate from 2007 to 2009, and founded the Roald Dahl Funny Prize in 2008 as part of his laureateship to honour books that make children laugh!

Go to michaelrosen.co.uk and click on 'videos' to find Michael doing 'Chocolate Cake' and many others.

QUENTIN BLAKE is one of Britain's most renowned illustrators. Born in the suburbs of London in 1932, he read English at Cambridge before becoming a full-time freelance illustrator. He began his career working for magazines such as *The Spectator* and *Punch*. For many years he taught at the Royal College of Art, where he was head of the Illustration Department from 1978 to 1986. He became the very first Children's Laureate in 1999 and was made a CBE in 2005. In 2013 he became Sir Quentin Blake when he was knighte[...]   [...]st.

Books by Michael Rosen

CENTRALLY HEATED KNICKERS
MICHAEL ROSEN'S BIG BOOK OF BAD THINGS
MICHAEL ROSEN'S BOOK OF VERY
SILLY POEMS (Ed.)
QUICK, LET'S GET OUT OF HERE
YOU WAIT TILL I'M OLDER THAN YOU
NO BREATHING IN CLASS
(with Korky Paul)

For Brian, Harold and remembering Connie

For Susanna, Joe and Eddie

Contents

QUICK, LET'S GET OUT OF HERE

Once I was round a friend's place
and just as we were going out
he went over to the table
and picked a hard lump of chewed-up
chewing gum with teeth marks in it
off the table top
and stuffed it in his mouth.

His gran was there and she said,
'You're not taking that filthy thing
with you, are you?'
And he said to me,
'Quick – let's get out of here.'

TRICKS

Nearly every morning
my brother would lie in bed,
lift his hands up in the air
full stretch
then close his hands around an invisible bar.
'Ah, my magic bar,' he'd say.
Then he'd heave on the bar,
pull himself up,
until he was sitting up in bed.

Then he'd get up.
I said,
'You haven't got a magic bar above your bed.'
'I have,' he said.
'You haven't,' I said.
'Don't believe me then,' he said.
'I won't – don't worry,' I said.
'It doesn't make any difference to me
if you do or you don't,' he said,
and went out of the room.

'Magic bar!' I said.
'Mad. He hasn't got a magic bar.'
I made sure he'd gone downstairs,
then I walked over to his bed
and waved my hand about in the air
above his pillow.
'I knew it,' I said to myself.
'Didn't fool me for a moment.'

WASHING UP

On Sundays,
my mum and dad said,
'Right, we've cooked the dinner,
you two can wash it up,'
and then they went off to the front room.

So then we began.
First there was the row about who
was to wash and who was to dry.
My brother said, 'You're too slow at washing,
I have to hang about waiting for you,'
so I said,
'You always wash, it's not fair.'

'Hard cheese,' he says,
'I'm doing it.'
So that was that.

'Whoever dries has to stack the dishes,'
he says,
so that's me stacking the dishes
while he's getting the water ready.

Now,
quite often we used to have mustard
with our Sunday dinner
and we didn't have it out of a tube,
one of us used to make it with the powder
in an eggcup
and there was nearly always
some left over.

Anyway,
my brother
he'd be washing up by now
and he's standing there at the sink
his hands in the water,
I'm drying up,
and suddenly he goes,

'Quick, quick quick
come over here
quick, you'll miss it,
quick, you'll miss it.'
'What?' I say, 'What?'
'Quick, quick. In here,
in the water.'
I say,

'What? What?'
'Give us your hand,' he says
and he grabs my hand
then my finger,
'What?' I say,
'That,' he says,
and he pulls my finger under the water
and stuffs it into the eggcup
with leftover blobs of old mustard
stuck to the bottom.
It's all slimey.
'Oh horrible.'

I was an idiot to have believed him.
So I go on drying up.

Suddenly
I feel a little speck of water on my neck.
I look up at the ceiling.
Where'd that come from?

I look at my brother –
he's grinning all over his big face.

'Oy, cut that out.'
He grins again
sticks his finger under the water
in the bowl and
flicks.
Plip.
'Oy, that got me right on my face.'
'Did it? Did it? Did it?'
He's well pleased.

So now it's my turn.
I've got the drying up cloth, haven't I?
And I've been practising for ages
on the kitchen door handle.
Now he's got his back to me
washing up
and

out goes the cloth, like a whip, it goes
right on the –
'Ow – that hurt. I didn't hurt *you*.'
Now it's me grinning.

So he goes,
'All right, let's call it quits.'
'OK,' I say, 'one–all. Fairy squarey.'

So I go on drying up.
What I don't know is that
he's got the Fairy Liquid bottle under the
water
boop boop boop boop boop boop
it's filling up
with dirty soapy water
and next thing it's out of the water
and he's gone squeeeesh
and squirted it right in my face.

'Got you in the mush,' he goes.

'Right, that's it,' I say,
'I've had enough.'
And I go upstairs and get
this old bicycle cape I've got,
one of those capes you can wear
when you ride a bicycle in the rain.

So I come down in that
and I say,
'OK I'm ready for anything you've got now.
You can't get me now, can you?'
So next thing he's got the little
washing-up brush
and it's got little bits of meat fat
and squashed peas stuck in it
and he's come up to me
and he's in, up, under the cape with it

working it round and round
under my jumper, and under my chin.

So that makes me really wild
and I make a grab for anything that'll
hold water; dip it in the sink
and fling it at him.

What I don't know is that
while I went upstairs to get the cape
he's got a secret weapon ready.

It's his bicycle pump –
he's loaded it with the dirty washing-up water
by sucking it all in.
He picks it up,
and it's squirt again.
All over my hair.

Suddenly the door opens.
'Have you finished the . . . ?'
It's Mum AND Dad.

'Just look at this.
Look at the pair of them.'

And there's water all over the floor
all over the table
and all we've washed up is
two plates and the mustard pot.

My dad says,
'You can't be trusted to do anything you're asked,
can you.'

He always says that.

Mind you, the floor was pretty clean
after we had mopped it all up.

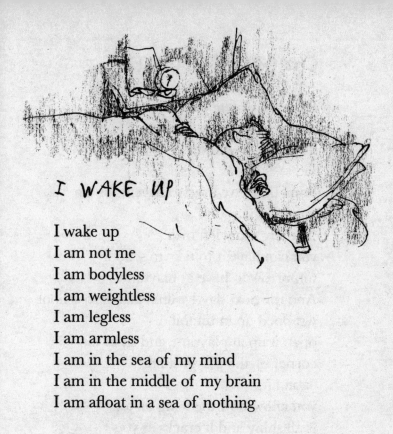

I WAKE UP

I wake up
I am not me
I am bodyless
I am weightless
I am legless
I am armless
I am in the sea of my mind
I am in the middle of my brain
I am afloat in a sea of nothing

It lasts for one flicker
of one eyelash

and then
once again
I am my full heaviness
I am my full headedness
I am my full bodyness
here.
Hallo.

CHOCOLATE CAKE

I love chocolate cake.
And when I was a boy
I loved it even more.

Sometimes we used to have it for tea
and Mum used to say,
'If there's any left over
you can have it to take to school
tomorrow to have at playtime.'
And the next day I would take it to school
wrapped up in tin foil
open it up at playtime and sit in the
corner of the playground
eating it,
you know how the icing on top
is all shiny and it cracks as you
bite into it
and there's that other kind of icing in
the middle
and it sticks to your hands and you
can lick your fingers
and lick your lips
oh it's lovely.
yeah.

Anyway,
once we had this chocolate cake for tea
and later I went to bed
but while I was in bed
I found myself waking up
licking my lips
and smiling.
I woke up proper.
'The chocolate cake.'
It was the first thing
I thought of.
I could almost see it
so I thought,
what if I go downstairs
and have a little nibble, yeah?
It was all dark
everyone was in bed
so it must have been really late
but I got out of bed,
crept out of the door

there's always a creaky floorboard, isn't there?

Past Mum and Dad's room,

careful not to tread on bits of broken toys
or bits of Lego
you know what it's like treading on Lego

with your bare feet,

yowwww
shhhhhhh

downstairs
into the kitchen
open the cupboard
and there it is
all shining.

So I take it out of the cupboard
put it on the table
and I see that
there's a few crumbs lying about on the plate,
so I lick my finger and run my finger all over
    the crumbs
scooping them up
and put them into my mouth.

ooooooooommmmmmmmm

nice.

Then
I look again
and on one side where it's been cut,
it's all crumbly.

So I take a knife
I think I'll just tidy that up a bit,
cut off the crumbly bits
scoop them all up
and into the mouth

oooooommm mmmm
nice.

Look at the cake again.

That looks a bit funny now –
one side doesn't match the other . . .
I'll just even it up a bit, eh?

Take the knife
and slice.
This time the knife makes a little cracky noise
as it goes through that hard icing on top.

A whole slice this time,

into the mouth.

Oh the icing on top
and the icing in the middle
ohhhhhh oooo mmmmmm.

But now
I can't stop myself.
Knife –
I just take any old slice at it
and I've got this great big chunk
and I'm cramming it in
what a greedy pig
but it's so nice,

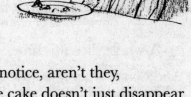

and there's another
and another and I'm squealing and
    I'm smacking my lips
and I'm stuffing myself with it
and
before I know
I've eaten the lot.
The whole lot.
I look at the plate.
It's all gone.

Oh no
they're bound to notice, aren't they,
a whole chocolate cake doesn't just disappear
does it?

What shall I do?

I know. I'll wash the plate up,

and the knife

and put them away and maybe no one
will notice, eh?

So I do that
and creep creep creep
back to bed
into bed
doze off
licking my lips
with a lovely feeling in my belly.
Mmmmmmmmmm.

In the morning I get up,
downstairs,
have breakfast,
Mum's saying,
'Have you got your dinner money?'
and I say,
'Yes.'
'And don't forget to take some chocolate cake
    with you.'
I stopped breathing.

'What's the matter,' she says,
'you normally jump at chocolate cake?'

I'm still not breathing,
and she's looking at me very closely now.
She's looking at me just below my mouth.
'What's that?' she says.
'What's what?' I say.
'What's that there?'
'Where?'
'There,' she says, pointing at my chin.
'I don't know,' I say.
'It looks like chocolate,' she says.
'It's not chocolate cake is it?'
No answer.
'Is it?'
'I don't know.'
She goes to the cupboard
looks in, up, top, middle, bottom,
turns back to me.
'It's gone.
It's gone.
You haven't eaten it, have you?'
'I don't know.'
'You don't know? You don't know if you've eaten
    a whole
chocolate cake or not?
When? When did you eat it?'

So I told her,

and she said
well what could she say?
'That's the last time I give you any cake to take
to school.
Now go. Get out
no wait
not before you've washed your dirty sticky face.'
I went upstairs
looked in the mirror
and there it was,
just below my mouth,
a chocolate smudge.
The giveaway.
Maybe she'll forget about it by next week.

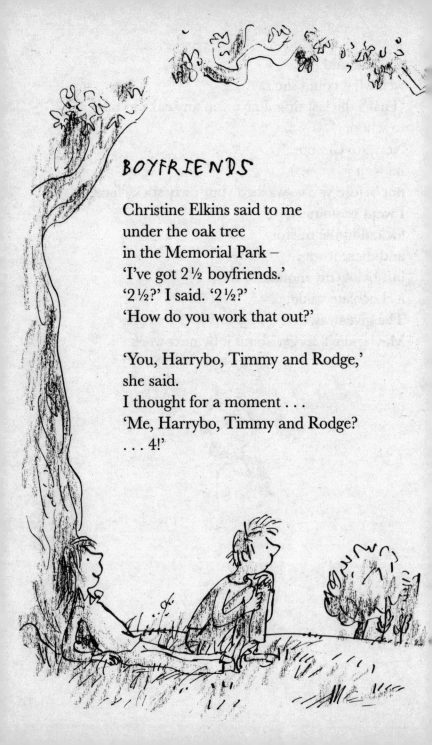

BOYFRIENDS

Christine Elkins said to me
under the oak tree
in the Memorial Park –
'I've got 2½ boyfriends.'
'2½?' I said. '2½?'
'How do you work that out?'

'You, Harrybo, Timmy and Rodge,'
she said.
I thought for a moment . . .
'Me, Harrybo, Timmy and Rodge?
. . . 4!'

I was just about to say,
'But that makes 4 –'
when suddenly I thought,
'She has halves – HALF boyfriends! . . .
. . . 2 halves make one? No. 3 halves plus 1 . . . yes.
'But, which ones are the halves?' I thought . . .
'and who's The One –
THE One?'

I never dared ask her
so I never found out.

MAD MEALS

Grilled cork
Matchbox on toast
glass soup
roasted clock
ping-pong ball and chips
Acorn sandwich
fillet of calculator
trouser salad
grilled lamp-post
ice cream (vanilla, soap or pepper)

MAD DRINKS

fizzy mouse
hot petrol
paint shake

MYSTERY

CRASH!!!

DAD: What was that noise?

SON: The bowl. I've broken the bowl.

MUM: What bowl?

SON: The one with lines on.

DAD: How did you break it?

SON: I was balancing it on my head.

DAD: The boy's mad.

MUM: How else is he going to practise?

DAD: Why were you balancing it on your head?

SON: I was pretending it was a hat.

DAD: Why do you need to practise pretending a bowl is a hat?

SON: (NO ANSWER)

I KNOW SOMEONE

I know someone who can
take a mouthful of custard and blow it
down their nose.
I know someone who can
make their ears wiggle.
I know someone who can
shake their cheeks so it sounds
like ducks quacking.
I know someone who can
throw peanuts in the air and catch them
in their mouth.
I know someone who can
balance a pile of twelve 2p pieces on his elbow
and snatch his elbow from under them
and catch them.
I know someone who can
bend her thumb back to touch her wrist.

I know someone who can
crack his nose.
I know someone who can
say the alphabet backwards.
I know someone who can put their hands in
their armpits and blow raspberries.
I know someone who can
wiggle her little toe.
I know someone who can
lick the bottom of her chin.
I know someone who can
slide their top lip one way
and their bottom lip the other way.
and that someone is
ME.

THIRTY-TWO LENGTHS

One Tuesday when I was about
ten
I swam thirty-two lengths
which is one mile.
And when I climbed out of the
water
I felt like a big, fat lump of jelly
and my legs were like rubber
and there was this huge man
there
with tremendous muscles all
over him
and I went up to him and said,
'I've just swum a mile.'
And he said,
'How many lengths was that
then?'
'Thirty-two,' I said.
And the man looked into the
water and said,
'I've got a lad here who can
do ninety.'

EDDIE IN BED

Sometimes I look really tired,
because you see
when most people are fast asleep
and I'm fast asleep
I hear,
'Waaaaaaaaaaaaaaaaaaaaaaaaaa.'
That's the baby, Eddie.
So I get out of bed and go into his room
and he's sitting up in bed
and he has these nightmares.
Not nightmares like you have,
like Dracula biting your head off or something.
He has nightmares about people taking food away
    from him.
So one night I go in there
and he's sitting up in bed
lifting his arms above his head
and banging them down
screaming,
'I want my biscuits I want my biscuits.'

Now if you can imagine that,
you can also imagine
that at this time he was sleeping
in the same bed as his brother.
Who was six.

And you have to imagine his brother's head
is right next to Eddie's hip.
Think about it.
Eddie's hands go above his head and
Wham
down by his side
right on Joe's head.
'I want my biscuits I want my biscuits.'
So Joe lifts his head and he goes,
'What's going on?'
Wham
'I want my biscuits.'
'What's going on?'
Wham
'I want my biscuits.'
'What's going on?'
Wham
'I want my biscuits.'
'Stop it, Eddie' – wham back
'I want my biscuits.'
Wham.
'OK, fellas,' I say,
'Cut it out.'
And I lift Eddie up and I take him into our bed.

What a stupid thing to do.

You see
most people sleep with their head
on the pillow
and their feet at the other end of the bed.
When Eddie comes into our bed
he sleeps with his head next to Susanna's head
and his feet in my ear.

And you have to imagine those feet
sticking in my ear.
And the toes.
Those toes are going
wiggle wiggly wiggly
Down my ear.
All night.
So by the time I get up
in the morning
I'm very tired
and very cross.

But I can always get my own back on him
in the morning
cos he hates having his nappy done . . .

GOING THROUGH THE OLD PHOTOS

Me, my dad
and my brother,
we were looking through the old photos.
Pictures of my dad with a broken leg
and my mum with big flappy shorts on
and me on a tricycle
when we got to one of my mum
with a baby on her knee,
and I go,
'Is that me or Brian?'
And my dad says,
'Let's have a look.
It isn't you or Brian,' he says.

32

'It's Alan.
He died.
He would have been
two years younger than Brian
and two years older than you.
He was a lovely baby.'

'How did he die?'
'Whooping cough.
I was away at the time.
He coughed himself to death in Connie's arms.
The terrible thing is,
it wouldn't happen today,
but it was during the war, you see,
and they didn't have the medicines.
That must be the only photo
of him we've got.'

Me and Brian
looked at the photo.
We couldn't say anything.
It was the first time we had ever heard about Alan.
For a moment I felt ashamed
like as if I had done something wrong.
I looked at the baby trying to work out
who he looked like.
I wanted to know what another brother
would have been like.

No way of saying.
And Mum looked so happy.
Of course she didn't know
when they took the photo
that he would die, did she?

Funny thing is,
though my father mentioned it every now and then
over the years,
Mum – never.
And he never said anything in front of her
about it
and we never let on that we knew.
What I've never figured out
was whether
her silence was because
she was more upset about it
than my dad –
or less.

EDDIE AND THE WALLPAPER

Eddie's always asking me to sing to him
and I'm hopeless at singing.
He'll find that out one day.
So he goes,
'Song. More.'
So I go, 'What song?'
So he goes,
'Song er man.'
So I have to sing,
'There was an old man called Michael Finnegan
He grew whiskers on his chinnegan
the wind came out and blew them in again
poor old Michael Finnegan, begin again.'

The bit that he likes best is that bit about
whiskers on his chinnegan.

If you could see my beard you'd know why.

So I go?
'There was an old man called . . .'
and up come the fingers . . .
'And he grew whiskers . . .'
and he grabs hold of my beard
and hangs on to it.
It really hurts you know.
'Stop it stop it. I won't go on.'

Then he lets go.
I carry on
and when I get to,
'The wind came out and *blew* them in again . . .'
he blows in my face with a great big
'PHOOOOOR'.
And you know babies are, all dribbly . . .
DIS
gusting.

So the other day he says
he wants a song about wallpaper.
Now you may think
why does he want a song about wallpaper?
There's a story behind it.
You see, not long ago we did some decorating.
When I say *we* did some
I'm lying.
Susanna did it and I just stood
at the bottom of the ladder.

Anyway, we were very pleased,
we came downstairs to have a cup of tea.
Eddie is off somewhere round the house.
He roams round the house on his own
like a free-range gorilla.

Sometimes you hear this huge crashing noise
    upstairs
and you know that's him jumping up and down
on the settee.
He doesn't think it's a settee –
he thinks it's a trampoline.
'Yippee yippee yippee.'

Anyway,
so we were there having tea
and Susanna says,
'Let's go and look at the wallpaper upstairs.'
So we go up there,
open the door,
and there's Eddie,
big smile on his face,
and he goes, 'Eddie helping.'
Oh no.
You know what that means . . .
TROUBLE.
It's like when you're putting tomato sauce
on his chips and he goes, 'Eddie helping,'

and next minute he's got hold of the sauce bottle
splodge splodge splodge
and you've got tomato sauce all over the table.

Well I'm looking at Eddie
and you know
when you do the decorating
you start at the top and you put the wallpaper *on*.
Well, Eddie started at the bottom
and took it *off*.
He had ripped the wallpaper off the wall.

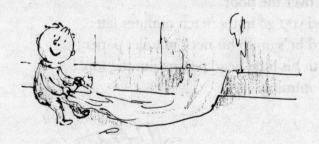

I think he thought it was like toilet paper.
He sometimes goes into the toilet

and he sees the toilet roll there
and he thinks,
well, that toilet roll looks dead boring
all rolled up there.
So he gets hold of one end of it
and he starts pulling it.
A bit more a bit more
and he's pulling and pulling the paper off the roll.

'Yippee yippee yippee,'
until he's pulled the whole toilet roll out
all over the floor
and you go in there ten minutes later
and he's up to his neck in toilet paper
with his little head poking out the top.
Swimming.

So that was why he wanted a song about wallpaper.
Maybe he thought wallpaper was a kind of
coloured toilet paper you stick to the wall.

THE WATCH

My mum and dad gave me a watch.
Not a posh watch,
good enough to tell the time by, though.
And it went well enough
until one day at a camp
we were playing smugglers and customs
over the sand dunes.

I was a smuggler
and I had to get £20,000
through the customs
for us to win the game.
£20,000 written on a piece of paper.
There were three ways to get past
the customs.
One – by running so fast
the customs couldn't catch you.
Two – by going creepy-crawly so they couldn't see you.
Three – going through the customs
with it hidden somewhere.

I chose three.
I chose to hide it on me somewhere.
But where?
'I know,' I said,
'I'll stuff it in my watch,'
and I took the back off my watch
folded up the piece of paper
with £20,000 written on it
and clipped the back of my watch on.

So then I went creepy-crawly over the sand dunes.

They saw me
they grabbed me
and they searched me.
They looked in my pockets
they looked in my shoes
they looked in my socks
they looked up my jumper
down my jumper
down my shirt
in my armpits.

They even looked *under* my watch
but they never thought to look
in my watch, did they?

So they let me go –

and when I got to the other end
where the other smugglers were
I said,
'Hooray, I got through.'
I opened up the back of my watch
and there it was –
£20,000.
I took it out – handed it over
and we had won the game.
I snapped the back of my watch on –
looked at the time and –
my watch. It had stopped.
It was broken.
I had broken it.

That evening I told my brother all about it
and I said,

'Don't tell Mum or Dad about it
or I'll get into trouble.
I'll get it mended secretly.'

So there we were, tea-time
and my brother suddenly goes,
'What's the time, Mick?'
and I went all red and flustered
and I go,
'Er er,'
and I look at my watch
and I go,
'Er er about six o'clock.'
'No it's not,' says my dad.
'It's seven o'clock,'
and he sees me going red.
'Is your watch going wrong?'
'Er – no.'
'Let's have a look.'
'No, it's all right.'
'Let me have a look. It's stopped,
it's broken. How did it get broken?'
'I don't know.'
'What do you mean you don't know.'

My brother was laughing all over his big face
without making a sound.

So then I told my dad
all about the smugglers and customs
and hiding the money in my watch.

He was furious.
'We gave you the watch
so you could tell the time
not for you to use as part of a secret agent's
smuggling outfit.
Well, don't expect us to buy you
presents like that again.'

I was *so* angry with my brother
for getting me into trouble.
Inside I was bubbling.
So –
as soon as tea was over
I went down to our backyard
where there was an old cherry tree
and I broke a twig off it.
It was all prickly and flakey
and covered in a kind of grey slimy muck.

So then I took this twig back upstairs
into our bedroom
and I'll tell you what I did with it.
I shoved it into his bed.
And as I shoved it into his bed

I thought
'This'll pay him back.
This'll pay him back.
This'll pay him back.

He's going to get into bed tonight
after I'm asleep
and his feet
are going to get all
prickled up
and covered in grey mucky slimy stuff.'

Well, later that evening
I was doing some homework
and I had some really hard sums to do.
I couldn't do them.
I was stuck
and my brother – he sees me
scribbling out all these numbers
and the page is a mess
so my brother, he says,
'What's up? Do you want a bit of help
with your sums?'
What could I say to that?
At first, I go,
'No no, it's all right.'
But he goes,
'No, come on – I'll lend you a hand.'

So I say, 'OK,'
and he comes over and he helped me.
He's sitting there right next to me,
my enemy,
showing me how to do my sums.
Then he said,
'Now you try,'
and then *I* could do them.

So there I was, friends with him,
grateful,
I'm saying, 'Thanks. Thanks for helping me.'

But in the back of my mind,
I know something:
THE TWIG WAS STILL IN THE BED.

I didn't know what to say.
All I could see was

THE TWIG
sitting in his bed
just where his feet would get it.

Even if I went and got it out

there'd still be a heap of dirty prickly bits
left in his bed,
after he's showed me how to get
all the sums right.

So I go,
'Look – when you go to bed –
tonight
there'll be a twig in your bed.'

So he goes,
'A twig in my bed? A twig in my bed?
How did it get there then?'

So I say,
'I put it there.'
And my mum and dad heard that.
So my dad goes,
'You put a twig in his bed?
Did I hear that right?
You put a twig in his bed, might I ask
Why did you put a twig in his bed?'

And I just couldn't say.
I just sat there like a lemon.
I couldn't say it was to pay him back for
telling on me about the watch
because they wouldn't think there was anything
    wrong
with him doing that.
So I just sat there
and then I said,
'I don't know.'
What a stupid thing to say.
My dad goes,
'You don't know why you put a twig in his bed?
You don't know why?
The boy's going mad.

First thing he does is smash up his watch
and next thing
he's going round stuffing a twig in people's beds.
He's going stark staring mad, I tell you.'

I didn't think I was going mad.
And I don't think my brother did.

I bet *he* knew why I put
a twig in his bed . . .

LIZZIE

When I was eleven
there was Lizzie.
I used to think this:

You don't care, Lizzie,
you say
that you're a ginger-nut
and you don't care.

I've noticed
that they try to soften you up

they say
you're clumsy

they say
you can't wear shorts
to school

but you say,
'I don't care,
I mean
how can I play football
in a skirt?'

Lizzie,
I'm afraid of saying
I think you're great

because, you see,
the teachers call you
tomboy.

I'm sorry
but I make out as if
I agree with the teachers
and the other girls
wear bracelets
and I've noticed
they don't shout like you
or whistle,
and, you see,
the other boys
are always talking about

those girls
with the bracelets
so I do too.

So I know
that makes me a coward
but that's why I don't dare
to say you're great,

but I think it to myself
when you're there
but I don't say.

I just try to show
I like you
by laughing
and joking about
and pulling mad faces.

I'm sorry
but I don't suppose
you'll ever know . . .

EDDIE AND THE GERBILS

Not long ago
we went on holiday with some people
who've got gerbils.
We haven't got any pets
and Eddie (he was two years old)
he thought they were
WONDERFUL.
He was always looking in their cage
going,
'Hallo gerbils, hallo gerbils, hallo gerbils.'
And when the boys took them out of the cage
Eddie loved stroking them,
going,
'Hallo gerbils, hallo gerbils, hallo gerbils,'
all over again.

Now,
when we got home from the holiday
Like I said,
we haven't got any pets.
What we've got, is
MICE.

So we wanted to get rid of them.
So we rang up the council to ask for the mouse-man
to come over and get rid of them.
The mouse-man.
That's not a man who is a mouse.
Silly,
it's a man who comes over
and he goes round
sniffing along the walls
and behind cupboards
to find where the mice go.

Then he puts down these little trays of poison,
only the mice don't know it's poison,
they think it's some really nice stuff
like biscuits.
And this poison
it burns them up from the inside
And they just die.
The dead ones pong a bit.
The bloke puts down little trays of this poison
and the mice find it and go,
'Wow. This looks really tasty stuff,'
gobble gobble gobble
clunk. Dead.
gobble gobble gobble

clunk.

So one morning we're having breakfast
and when Eddie has breakfast
sometimes he sits at the table
sometimes he sits on the table
sometimes he sits under the table.
Well,
this particular morning
he was sitting under the table.

So I'm eating my breakfast
munch munch munch
and suddenly I hear
'Hallo gerbils.'
'Uh?' Ignore it. Munch munch munch.
'Hallo gerbils.'
Better have a look.
Oh no.
He's got a dead mouse in his hand.
Clutching it.
Head poking out the top of his fist
tail out the bottom.
And he's stroking it.
The dead mouse.
And he's going,
'Hallo gerbils hallo gerbils hallo gerbils.'

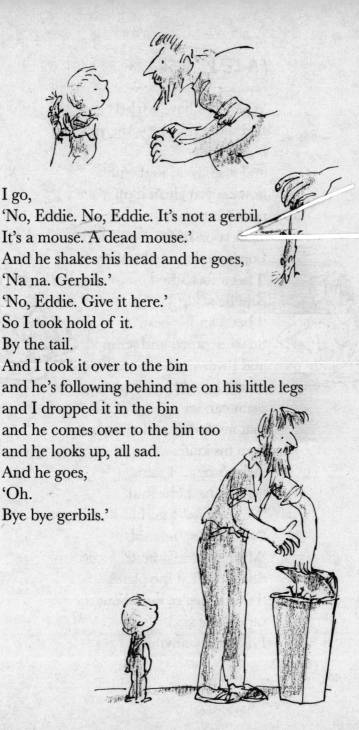

I go,
'No, Eddie. No, Eddie. It's not a gerbil.
It's a mouse. A dead mouse.'
And he shakes his head and he goes,
'Na na. Gerbils.'
'No, Eddie. Give it here.'
So I took hold of it.
By the tail.
And I took it over to the bin
and he's following behind me on his little legs
and I dropped it in the bin
and he comes over to the bin too
and he looks up, all sad.
And he goes,
'Oh.
Bye bye gerbils.'

FRIED EGG

When you have a fried egg
and the yellow bit – the yolk –
is all runny
and it spills on to the plate,
how do you clean it off your
plate?
With your knife or your fork?
I once said to my brother,
'I bet a fork's best.'
And he said,
'I bet a knife's best.'
So we scraped and scraped
and I was sure,
in fact I could see as plain as
plain can see
that my fork had done it better
than his knife.
'Mine's best,' I said.
'Mine's best,' he said.
'No mine is,' I said.
'No mine is,' he said.
'Mum, whose is best?' I said.
She looked at the plates.
'I think they're just about the
same,' she said.
I didn't say anything,

I just knew that she was wrong.
My fork was better than his
knife for getting
egg yolk off plates.
It was as simple as that.
It made me so angry.
I thought,
'Why doesn't he admit it?
I know he knows mine is best.'

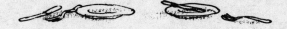

BATHTIME

Quite often
my mum used to say to me:
'Isn't it time you had a bath?'
and I'd say:
'But I had one yesterday.'
'No you didn't,' she'd say.
'Well – the day before yesterday, then,' I'd say.
'Right,' she says – 'I'll run the water.
You be ready to get in when it's full.'

So when
the bathroom was full of steam
I was ready to climb in.
One thing though –
I never get into a bath
bold and bare all over. You see,
a bath is part of the water world
and I always like to keep in touch with the dry
world
till the last possible moment.
So what I do is take off all my clothes
except my vest.
I step over and in – how's that? Owah!
as hot as feet can bear.
I kneel down
as hot as knees can bear. Oh!

Down a bit, down a bit
as hot as bottom can bear. Oooph!
Sit for one moment in the water world
with my last dry thing still on –
then, vest off, over the edge, out of sight
and I slide the rest of me into the water.

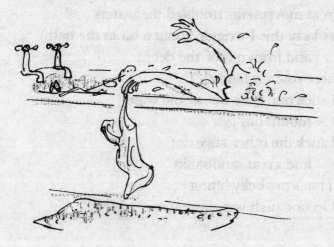

I have stepped from the dry world to the wet world.
I am now a water beast.
I'm miles away from dry places like
blankets and dust,
carpets, hats and paper,
straw and cake.
I'm a wet thing that slips and slides,
lips that burble in the ripples.
My skin can shine like fish
and my hands can twist the water into ringlets
that show up on the bottom of the bath.
I am a wet thing.
It's films time; I say:
'There was once a time
when the whole world was water,
and it was all still. But then –
beneath the surface,
great movements troubled the waters . . .'
(as I say this I wriggle about a bit in the bath)
'. . . and from out of the deeps –
there rose – islands . . .'
(I stick one knee out of the water)
'. . . mountains . . .'
(I stick the other knee out)
'. . . and great sandbanks.'
(That's my belly lifting.)
'On one such wet shore came – LIFE.'

(I make my fingers walk out of the water
and across my belly.)

The steam
has now settled on the walls
and there are dots of water there,
getting together, ganging up,
becoming drips.
Drips get too big to stop where they are
and slip.

Now,
what if I helped a gang of dots
with a flick of water from out of the bath?
Flick my finger and thumb. PLIP!
and the dots become a drip,
the drip begins to slip.
Another PLIP! More dots become a drip –
another drip begins to slip.

It's a race!
'Welcome back to Bathroom for the
Big Downfall Drip Race . . .

and it's Dropso – yes it's Dropso
away to a great start well ahead from
Longbottom with the long bottom
in second place near the pipes.

It's Dropso from Longbottom. Dropso from
    Longbottom.
Dropso in fine form

heading hard for a gang of dots.
Longbottom behind – slow but steady
taking in the dots one by one,
Dropso fairly tearing down the wall has –
no, yes, no –
swung sideways, staggered across the wall,
dived into another gang of dots
and is now, is now bulged up like a ripe plum
ready to plunge to victory –
Longbottom still slow. Still oh so slow.
No. I lie.
Plucky little Longbottom with the long bottom
picking up now, picking up dots
picking up – bulging, bulging.
Old Dropso has stuck. Is this wise?

And it's plucky Longbottom gushing like a very
  mountain
torrent
now closing up the gap on the drooping Dropso.
This could be dangerous.
Longbottom nosediving right on to droopy
  Dropso's tracks.

Longbottom is slipping helplessly along Dropso's
  trail.
It's going to be a crash.
It *is* a crash.
Longbottom has dropped on to Dropso. It's a
  drop-on.
A drop-on. What a scene! Fantastic.
What an end –
no race but plenty of thrills.

From Bathroom – back to you in London.'
Now where's that flannel?
On with more bathtime business.
Watch this!

You take the flannel.
Open it up square.
Hang it up from its corners
    in front of you,
with both hands – like a picture.
Then, flop it down
flat smack on the water to float.
Now take one hand beneath the surface of the
water
under the flannel.
Point your fingers upwards,
make your hand like a tower.
Lift this tower-hand up into the floating flannel.
Lift the flannel just a bit out of the water.
Stop.
Feel the flannel suck round your fingers.
Looks a bit like a head – someone swimming?
With a head scarf on . . .
Now, grab the flannel head round its neck.

'Help! It's a snake. It's got me round the neck.
    Aaargh.'
'What did you say?'
'Aaaargh.'

The snake drags the head slowly down below the
    surface.

Take your free hand – the one that isn't the snake.
Grab the head, now it's underwater and –
    squeeze.
All the air trapped in the flannel bubbles up.
Blubble bubble bulbybobble
bopbopbopbopbopbop.

'You remember JAWS – THE TERROR OF
    THE DEEP!
NOW! SNAKE – THE TERROR OF THE
    BATH!'

By now
after these adventures
there are colder currents in the bath.

So it's tidal wave time.
Get under and slide down the bath.

69

Slide back   slide down   slide back   down
  back

ffoom   ffomp   ffoom   ffomp   ffoom   ffomp

Big wave
to and fro and
grab the side. BRAKES ON.
'The two-hundred-foot wave engulfs the cold
water tap and the overflow hole.
Millions of gallons of seawater plunge over the
edge and cascades more pour out of the overflow
into the yard outside.'
Suddenly comes:
'Have you finished in there?'
The door opens. It's Mum.
'What are you doing?
The floor is covered in water and you haven't even
touched the soap.
You've been in here for nearly half an hour.
What have you been doing?'
'I was a snake. There was a race. And then there
was a tidal wave, Mum.'
'Well your father's just home and he says he got
soaked from the overflow pipe as he was coming in
    the door.'
'That was the tidal wave, Mum.'
'Oh was it? Now you get out of there quick or

you'll turn into a sponge.'
'Would I?'
'Well, look at your hands. You've begun already.
Now come on out of there.'
I look at them. She's right. They've turned into
wrinkly white sponges.
Just think of that.
Staying in a bath so long
you turn into a sponge.
It's time to come back to the dry world.
Towel, pyjamas, sheets, blankets.
Bed.

WISE ONE

Wise one, wise one
how long is a piece of string?

Twice as long as half its length.

Wise one, wise one
how do you kill a snake?

Put its tail in its mouth
and it'll eat itself up.

Wise one, wise one
What's at the end of cat's tail?

A cat.

Wise one, wise one
How can I get a chick out of a boiled egg?

Feed it to the chicken
so it can lay it again.

Wise one, wise one
Why do bricklayers put mortar on bricks?

To keep the bricks together
and to keep the bricks apart.

Wise one, wise one
My parrot talks too much.

Give it a good book to read.

GO-KART

Me and my mate Harrybo
we once made a go-kart.
Everyone was making go-karts
so we had to make one.

Big Tony's was terrific,
Big Tony was terrific
because Big Tony told us he was.
What he said was,
'I am TERRIFIC,'
And because Big Tony was VERY big
no one said,
'Big Tony.
You are NOT terrific.'
So,
Big Tony was terrific
and Big Tony's go-kart was terrific.
And that was that.

When Big Tony sat on his go-kart
he looked like a real driver.
He had control.
When he came down a road round our way
called Moss Lane
he could make the wind blow his hair,
pheeeeeeooooooooooph,
he could make the wheels of his go-kart go

prrrrrrrrrrrrrrrrr
and he went
eeeeeeeeeeeeooowwwwwww
as he went past.
I was jealous of Big Tony.
I was afraid that I thought
he might be
terrific.

So me and Harrybo
we made a go-kart
out of his old pram
and some boxes and crates
we got from the off-licence.
We nailed it up with bent nails
but Harrybo's dad said,
'No no no no no
you should use big metal staples,'
And he gave us some.
He said they were
Heavy Duty.

Heavy duty
wow
That sounded
terrific.

So then we tied cord round
    the front cross-piece.
But Harrybo's dad said,
'No no no no no,
you should use the pram handle.'
And he helped us fix
the pram handle to the cross-piece
He said, 'That'll give you
Control.'

Control
wow
That sounded
terrific.

Harrybo sat on the beer-crate
and steered,
I kneeled behind.
But Harrybo's dad said,
'No no no no no
you should kneel on foam pads.'
And he cut these two foam pads
for me to kneel on.
Harrybo's dad said,
'That'll help you
Last The Course.'

Last the course,
wow
That sounded
terrific.

Our go-kart was ready.

So we took it up to the top of Moss Lane
and Harrybo said,
'I'll steer,' and he did.
It was fan-
tastic.
It felt just like Big Tony looked.
The hair in the wind

pheeeeeeeooooooooooph
the wheels
prrrrrrrrrrrrrrrrr
and so we both went
eeeeeeeeeeeeeoooowwwwwwwwww

So we took it up to the top
of Moss Lane again
and Harrybo said,
'I'll steer,'
and he did.
It was a-
mazing.
The road went blurry.

The hair in the wind
pheeeeeeeoooooooph
the wheels went
prrrrrrrrrrrrrr

so we both went
eeeeeeeeeoooowwwwwwwww

So we took it up to the top of Moss Lane again
and Harrybo said,
'I'll steer,'
so I said,
'Can I have a go?'

Harrybo said,
'NO.'
'Go on,' I said.
'No,' he said, 'You've never done it.'
'Go on, Harrybo. Let me have a go.
Go on. I mean. Blimey.
Come on, Harrybo. Go on.'
'No.'
'Oh go on. Go on. Go on.'

'All right,' he said.
'Look out, won't you.'
'Yeah yeah yeah. *I* know,' I said.
I thought,
'I'm going to be
terrific.'
My hair – pheeeoooph
wheels – prrrrrr
me – eeeow

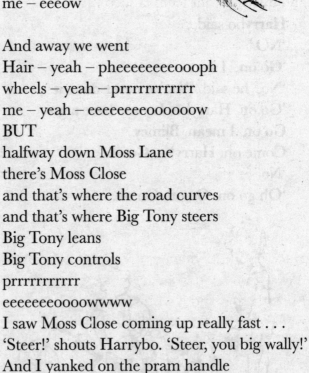

And away we went
Hair – yeah – pheeeeeeeeooooph
wheels – yeah – prrrrrrrrrrrr
me – yeah – eeeeeeeeooooooow
BUT
halfway down Moss Lane
there's Moss Close
and that's where the road curves
and that's where Big Tony steers
Big Tony leans
Big Tony controls
prrrrrrrrrrr
eeeeeeeooooowwww
I saw Moss Close coming up really fast . . .
'Steer!' shouts Harrybo. 'Steer, you big wally!'
And I yanked on the pram handle
uh
and the whole world

went round once and twice
and three times
and my head went rolling
down the road
pulling me after it
and the go-kart came for the ride
over and over and over
until my nose and my chin
and my two front teeth landed up
in the grit of the gutter.

Harrybo was crying.
'Wo wo wo oooo wo wo ooo.'
I breathed in and it whistled.
'Whew.'
'Whew.'
There it was again.
I stuck my finger up to my tooth
and it was chipped.

Harrybo said,
'Your chin's bleeding,'
and I said,
'Your chin's bleeding an' all.'
'I know ooooooo,' he said.

We walked home.
He pulled the kart,
got to his place
he didn't say anything.
Nothing at all.
Not a word.
And he went in.
I walked on to my place
'Whew – whew – whew,'
it was still whistling.

When I got in
I told Mum everything
and she said, well, she said all kinds of things –
like, 'Well – your teeth'll
probably fall out, you know.'
One of those nice things
that mums say.

Next day at school
they were all asking about the crash
they all looked at my tooth

and they all wanted to see the go-kart.
Harrybo said,
'You can't,
cos my dad's
chopped it up.'

Chopped up.
Wow
that sounded
terrible.

Hey,
when Harrybo got his racer,
his brand new racing bike for Christmas
I didn't ask him for a go on it.
I didn't
no
I didn't.

I wonder why.

END OF THE WORLD

Sometimes it looks as if it could be
the end of the world:

earthquakes
volcanoes
hurricanes
floods

sometimes it's lightning at night
and there's thunder in your ears.

It could be
the end of the world.

Sometimes you hear
small boys and girls
howling,

'I've dropped my lolleeeeeeeeeee,'
or
'He's got my sweeteeeeeeeeeeees,'

and Mum or Dad say to them:
'It's not the end of the world you know.'

They think it is.

BUBBE AND ZEYDE
(VISITING MUM'S MUM AND DAD)

We sometimes see them on Sunday.
They live in a dark room at the end of a dark corridor
and Bubbe kisses us all when we arrive.
She looks like Mum but very silver and bent at the middle,
which we will all look like one day says Mum's father.
Dad always looks fed up because he doesn't want to come
but Mum talks to them properly.
Zeyde looks tired
and pretends that the half crown he's going to give me
disappears into the ceiling along with my nose
if I'm not careful – snap – and there's his thumb in his fist,
and he beats me at draughts, dominoes, snap,
hare-and-hounds,
and even dice
and he's got a bottle with a boat in it
and we go for walks on Hackney Downs
which he calls Acknee Dans.

And all the old men there say, 'Hallo, Frank,'
and while we're walking along he says:
'What's to become of us, Mickie, what's to become of
us?'
and I don't know what to answer.

And he shows me to Uncle Hymie
who looked out of his window and said:
'Is that big boy your grandson, Frank?' (even though he
knows my name)
because that's the way they talk.
And when we get back we eat chopped herring or
chopped liver which is my favourite
and Bubbe tells stories that go on for hours
about people she knows who are ill or people who've
had to pay too much money and at the end of the story
it always seems as if she's been cheated.
And once she took a whole afternoon to tell Mum
how to make pickled cucumber and she kept saying:
'Just add a little salt to taste, a little salt to taste,
just taste it and see if there's enough salt,
to make sure if there's enough salt – just taste and see.'
And she calls me, 'Tottala,' and rubs my hair and bites
her lips as though I'm going to run away
and so she shakes her head and
says, 'Oy yoy yoy yoy yoy.'
But Zeyde goes to sleep in the old brown armchair
with his hands on the pockets of his flappy blue trousers

and when we go Mum frowns
and Zeyde holds my hand in his puffy old hand,
keeps ducking his head in little jerks
and says to us all, come again soon,
but I'd be afraid to go all the way on my own
and it's very dark and the lavatory is outside
which is sometimes cold.
She doesn't like it when we go,
and she kisses us all over again
and Dad walks up and down like he does at the station
and Mum keeps pushing me and poking me
and they both wave all the time we go away into the
distance
and I always wave back because I think they like it
but Mum and Dad sit absolutely quiet
and nobody speaks for ages.
Mum says Zeyde shouldn't give me the money.

EDDIE AND THE NAPPY

Eddie hates having his nappy done.
So I say all cheery,
'Time for your nappy, Eddie,'
and he says, all sad,
'No nappeee.'
And I say,
'Yes, nappy.'
So I have to run after him going,
'Nappy nappy nappy nappy . . .'

And he's got these little fat rubbery legs
that go round like wheels;
so away he runs
with a wicked grin on his face
screaming,
'Woooo woooo woooo.'

So I go running after him
shouting,
'Nappy nappy nappy,
I'll get you I'll get you . . .'
until I catch him.

Then I lift him up
lay him over my knees
to get his nappy off.

89

While I'm doing the pins
he gargles,
'Geereegreegeereegree,'
waving his podgy little legs in the air.
He thinks,
great. Time to kick Dad's chin.
And smack smack smack
on my chin.

When I've cleaned him up
it's time for the cream
You have to put cream on a baby's bum
or they get nappy rash.
But we leave the jar of cream
on the window sill
where it gets all cold.
So I go,
'Time for the cream, Eddie.'
And he goes,

'No cream.'
So I say,
'Yeah, cream,'
and I blob it on
and he goes, 'Oooh.'

You imagine what that would feel like.
A great blob of cold cream.
It would be like
having an ice lolly down your pants.

So then I put the nappy on
and away he goes on those little rubbery legs
going,
'Woooo woooo woooo.'

CLONKING ALL THE DRAINS

We're clonking
we're clonking
we're clonking all the drains.

We stamp on all the drain covers
even when it rains.

There's covers for the gas
there's covers for the drains
there's covers for the phone wires
and ones for water mains.

There's covers for the hole
where they used to put the coal.

And you can stamp on every one of them
round our way.
I stamped on a wobbly one
only today.

We're clonking
we're clonking
we're clonking all the drains.

We stamp on all the drain covers
even when it rains.

MONEY BOX

My first money box
was a yellow house
with a green roof.
On the roof
was a yellow woodpecker.
On the woodpecker there was
a green beak.
In his beak was
a slot.
In the slot,
went your money.
At that –
the yellow woodpecker pecked the chimney
on the green roof
of the yellow house
and the money rolled down the beak,
down the chimney
and into the house.
Eeeeeeeeewwwwwwww clunk.
Funny thing is:
I can't remember how I got the money out!

My next money box
was A Money Box.
A wooden box with a trick drawer.
You opened the drawer
you put the money in the drawer
you closed the drawer
and when you pulled the drawer out –
it was empty – the money was gone.
My friends came over.

'OK,' I said,
'you put your money in the drawer,
close the drawer,
pull the drawer out
and your money's gone.
It's in the box.'

'How does it work?'

'Not saying.'

'Well, I'm not putting my money in it then.'

'Well you won't see it work then, will you?'

'All right – one penny – there.'

'In goes the drawer, out it comes – see – the penny's gone.'

'How do I get it back then?'

'Secret.'

NEWCOMERS

My father came to England
from another country
My father's mother came to England
from another country
but my father's father
stayed behind.

So my dad had no dad here
and I never saw him at all.

One day in spring
some things arrived:
a few old papers,
a few old photos
and – oh yes –
a hulky bulky thick checked jacket
that belonged to the man
I would have called 'Grandad'.
The Man Who Stayed Behind.

But I kept that jacket
and I wore it
and I wore it
and I wore it
till it wore right through
at the back.

SKELETONS

My dad was in Berlin in 1946
    and his old friend David
    said that a friend of his
    was
    at The Berlin Natural History Museum.

    David wondered if he was still there.

At the time
Berlin was under a foot of snow,
the roads were covered with snow,
there was scarcely anything going along them.

You could scarcely see where the roads went.

    My dad says he walked for hours
    through heaps of bomb rubble and snow
    round huge craters in the ground
    under walls leaning over.

      Snow everywhere.
      Till suddenly, he came face to face with
      some enormous skeletons in the snow.

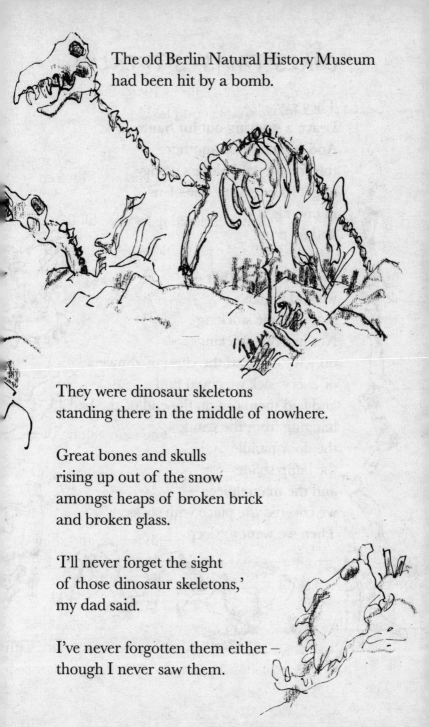

The old Berlin Natural History Museum
had been hit by a bomb.

They were dinosaur skeletons
standing there in the middle of nowhere.

Great bones and skulls
rising up out of the snow
amongst heaps of broken brick
and broken glass.

'I'll never forget the sight
of those dinosaur skeletons,'
my dad said.

I've never forgotten them either –
though I never saw them.

CHRISTMAS STOCKING

They say:
Leave a stocking out for Santa.
And somehow or another
this friendly old bloke's going
to get round every one of us
in one night
and fill it up.

Me and my brother –
we had a plan.
Not just one stocking
Not just two stockings
no – we emptied the chest of drawers
of every sock we could find
and laid them out on the end of the bed,
hanging from the window,
the door handle,
the lamp shade
and the mantelpiece –
we covered the place with socks.
Then we went to sleep.

I don't know what the old bloke thought
when he came
but he must have turned up and said:
'Well – that little show doesn't fool me,'
and he stuffed a few sweets in one sock
just one single solitary sock,
and left.

At least,
that's what Mum and Dad
thought he did.

MRS TOWNSEND

Every time I see Mrs Townsend
she says
Oh I remember you, you rascal
I can see it now
Your mum and dad was out
looking for you
you was only three
you had gone missing.

You know where they found you?
Halfway up the road
outside the methodist church
running along in your little vest
you didn't have nothing else on
you had left home
with just your vest on
everything else open to the weather
can you imagine?

Well you would never think of that
to look at you now,
would you?

NO

EDDIE AND THE BIRTHDAY

When Eddie had his second birthday
he got lots of cards,
and he had a cake and all kinds of presents
and we sang 'Happy Birthday'.
'Happy birthday to you
Happy birthday to you
Happy birthday, dear Eddie . . . '
and all that.
He liked that very much
So he goes:
'More. Sing it again.'
So we sang it again.
'Happy birthday to you
Happy birthday to you
Happy birthday, dear Eddie . . . '
and all that.
And he goes,
'More. Sing it again.'
So we sang it again.
'Happy birthday to you
da de da de da, dear Eddie
da de da to you . . . '
And he goes.
'More. Sing it again.'
It felt like we sang 'Happy Birthday' about
Two hundred and twenty-three times.

And the candles. On the cake.
He loved them.
'Eddie, blow.'
He blew.
And the moment he blew it out
he wanted more.

'More candle.'
So we light them.
'More Eddie blow.'
Eddie blew.
'More candle.'

We light.
'More Eddie blow.'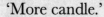
'More candle.'
That felt like two hundred and twenty-
three times as well.

And he loved the cards.
Everyone who sent him a card
seemed to think he'd like one
with pictures of big fat animals.

Elephants and hippos.
He got about ten of them.
Imagine.
Your second birthday
and everyone sends you pictures of
hippopotamuses.
Maybe they think he *is* a hippo.
Anyway he had a nice birthday.
Next day he gets up
comes downstairs
and he looks round

and he goes,
'More happy birfdy.'
So I go,
'That was yesterday, Eddie.'
'More happy birfdy.'
'But it isn't your birfdy – I mean birthday . . . '
'More happy birfdy.'

Now, you don't cross Eddie.
He has rages.
We call them wobblies.
'Look out, he's going to throw a wobbly!'
And the face starts going red,
the arms start going up and down,
the screaming starts winding up
he starts jumping up and down
and there he is –
throwing a wobbly.

So I thought,
'We don't want to have a wobbly over this one.'
So we started singing 'Happy Birthday' all over again.

Two hundred and twenty-three times.
Then he says
'More candles.'
'We haven't got any,' we say
(lies, of course, we had).
'More candles . . .'
So out came the candles
and yes –
'Eddie, blow.'
He blew.
'More candle.'
And off we go again –
Two hundred and twenty-three times.

And then he says,
'Letters, more.'
Well, of course no one sent him any more,
so while I'm singing more happy birfdys,
my wife was stuffing all the cards
into envelopes and sticking them down.
So we hand over all his cards again
and out came all the hippopotamuses again.

So he's very pleased.
And that's how Eddie had two birthdays.
Lucky for us
he'd forgotten by the third day.

Maybe he thinks when you're two you have two
birthdays
and when you're three you have three birthdays
and when you're seventy-eight you . . .

PLATFORM

I'm standing on platform one
of Pinner station
at half past four.

Mum comes at ten to five.

When I wait for her
I watch the signals for the express trains change
I watch the lights change
I watch the trains going dark as they
come under the bridge.

I'm waiting for my mum.

I go and stand by the
glass case on the wall
where the Christian Science people
put a Bible for you to read.
It's open and there are bits
of the page marked that you're
supposed to read.
I don't understand it.

I watch the woman in the sweety kiosk
serving people.
Mars bar, bar of plain chocolate,

packet of chewing gum, Mars bar, KitKat,
barley sugars.

Are you waiting for your mum again?

Yes.

I go and stand on the shiny floor of the waiting room
and look at the big dark benches. There's a boiler in there.
They never light it.
Even in winter.

There are big advertisements that I read.

One says:
'Children's shoes have far to go.'
And a boy and girl are walking away
down a long long road to nowhere

with thick woods on both sides of them.
I'm not waiting for a train
I'm waiting for my mum.

At a quarter to
The Flying Scotsman Express Train comes
through.
I stand back against the wall.
It's the loudest thing I know.
The station goes dark,
I stop breathing,
the coaches move so fast
you can't see the people in them.
At ten to five
Mum's there.

The doors open.
She'll be in the second carriage,
she always is.

Daylight shines from behind her
so I can't see her face
but I know it's her –
Mum.
I know it's her
by her shape
and her bag
and her walk.

Have you been waiting long?
No.
You could have gone home, you know. You've got
a key.

I like waiting for you.
It's better than being at home on my own.

I suppose it is.

I point to the children
in the big advertisement:
'Children's shoes have far to go.'

Where are they going, Mum?

I don't know.

I hold Mum's hand all the way home.

ON THE TRAIN

When you go on the train
and the line goes past the backs of houses in a town
you can see there's thousands and thousands
of things going on;
someone's washing up,
a baby's crying,
someone's shaving,
someone said, 'Rubbish, I blame the government.'
Someone tickled a dog,
someone looked out the window
and saw this train
and saw me looking at her
and she thought,
'There's someone looking out the window
looking at me.'

But I'm only someone
looking out the window
looking at someone
looking out the window
looking at someone.

Then it's all gone.

AUNTIE WINTERMIDDLE

When I was seven I made up my mind:
I am going to prove
once and for all
there is no such person as Father Christmas.
I'll stay up all night
and when he comes down the chimney
I'll say,
'There's no such person as Father Christmas.'
– no –
I mean no one'll come down the chimney
which will all go to show
that I'm right
and everyone else is wrong.

So that Christmas
the Christmas when I was seven
I went to bed
very very excited.
I lay in bed, my eyes wide open
staring up at the ceiling
staring at the door
staring at the fireplace
going,
'I'm not going to go to sleep
I'm not going to go to sleep.'
I went on like that for ages

and ages, hours and hours
until suddenly I heard
a rustling sound.
It was coming from the fireplace.
A bit of soot fell into the fireplace.
I sat up in bed
and stared into the dark.
Then slowly there appeared
feet, legs, body
then a whole person.
'Who is it?
Who is it?'
I called out in the dark.
No answer.
The shape moved across the room.
It tripped over my yellow dumper truck
that I had left there
just in case there *was* a Father Christmas
so he wouldn't leave me another yellow
dumper truck.

Anyway –
it turned on the light.
I blinked.
It was a woman.
'Hi,' she says,
'I'm Auntie Wintermiddle.'
'Auntie Winterpiddle?' I said.

'No, Auntie Wintermiddle.'

'What are you doing in my room,' I said.

'Well, Michael,' she said,

'I've come to give you your Wintermiddle
  presents.'

'How do you know my name?'

'I know everyone's name,' she said.

'Blimey,' I said.

'What do you want?' she said.

'An Action Man,' I said.

'I haven't got any dollies like that,' she said.

'Action Man isn't a dolly,' I said.

'Well I haven't got any Action Man dollies either.'

'I want a gun,' I said.

'I haven't got any guns,' she said.

'You're useless,' I said.

'Am I?' she said. 'Watch this, then.'

Her fingers turned into felt-tips
and paint brushes
and she was up the walls
across the ceiling
drawing, scribbling, colouring.
She did pictures of tigers, aliens,
roller-skaters, trees, dragons, aeroplane
cabins, skeletons, people, moons.
Fantastic.

She wrote on the door:
Knock knock
who's there?
Toodle
Toodle who?
Toodle-oo? But you've only just arrived.

She wrote:
Father Christmas is a fat fool
above the fireplace

She wrote:
What goes snap, crackle, squeak squeak
squeak?
Mice Crispies.

And she hung a giant paper sun
with a light inside it from the ceiling.

'How about that?' she said.
'All right,' I said.
'Not so bad actually.
What else can you do?'
'I can turn the world upside down.
How about that?'
'Like what?' I said.
'Follow me,' she said.
And she took me to the window.
Pow! a flash went out from her hand.
Night turned to day
and the cars parked in the street
turned into buses,
all shapes, sizes and colours
covered all over with mad faces
winking and smiling.
There were no cars just these buses,
some the shape of giant tortoises

and giant tins of baked beans
giant feet and giant doughnuts.

Pow!
the room, my room
turned into a hall,
so big it looked as if all the children of the
world could fit in it.
I don't suppose it was that big
but there were thousands of us
and we were all blowing up this
huge huge huge purple balloon.

We each had a bit to blow through
and we were blowing and blowing
and the balloon was getting bigger and bigger,
it was swelling up above our heads
and we were blowing and blowing
it was getting so big I thought it was
going to burst.

There we were, thousands and thousands of us
blowing and blowing
until I thought it really was going to burst
so I called out,
'Stop, stop, stop.'
And in a flash everything did stop.

There was a grinding, smashing roar,
light turned to dark
the hall shrank to a room – my room,
there was a sucking whooshing sound
and I saw Auntie Wintermiddle's feet
disappearing up the chimney.

'Come back, come back,' I shouted.
'Come back, Auntie.'
But there wasn't a sound,
and so, tired and sad – I fell asleep.

In the morning
there were presents.
Dad said, 'Look what Father Christmas brought
    you.'
'Did he?' I said.
'You believe in the old Father Christmas story,
    don't you?' he said.
'I know a better one,' I said.

'A better what?' he said.
'A better story,' I said.
'What's that?' said Mum.
'Oh – never mind,' I said.

But later that day
I went upstairs
and wrote underneath the mantelpiece
'I love Auntiewinterpiddle
– no sorry –
Auntiewintermiddle
I'll stay up for you next year.'

THE ITCH

If your hands get wet
in the washing-up water,
if they get covered in flour,
if you get grease or oil
all over your fingers,
if they land up in the mud,
wet grit, paint, or glue . . .

have you noticed
it's just then
that you always get
a terrible itch
just inside your nose?
And you can try to
twitch your nose,
twist your nose,
squeeze your nose,
scratch it with your arm,
scrape your nose on
your shoulder
or press it
up against the wall,
but it's no good.
You can't get rid of
the itch.
It drives you so mad

you just have to let a
finger get at it.
And before you know
you've done it.
You've wiped a load of glue,
or oil,
or cold wet pastry
all over the end of your nose.

ORANGE JUICE

We get orange juice
delivered to our door
with the milk,
on Mondays, Wednesdays and Fridays.
We get one pint of milk,
one carton of orange juice.

So,
one Monday morning
I go out there
and there's one pint of milk
and
no orange.

So I go,
'Damn – the milkman's
forgotten to deliver the orange.
I love orange juice for breakfast.'

So on Tuesday,
I got up in time to meet the milkman
and I say to him,
'Hey, you forgot to deliver the orange
yesterday.'
'No, I never,' he said.
'Afraid you did,' I said.

'I delivered your orange yesterday,' he says.
'Well it wasn't there when I came
to collect it.'
So I got another one off him.

On Wednesday,
same again,
one pint of milk
no orange.

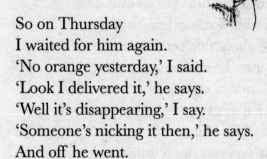

So on Thursday
I waited for him again.
'No orange yesterday,' I said.
'Look I delivered it,' he says.
'Well it's disappearing,' I say.
'Someone's nicking it then,' he says.
And off he went.

Suddenly,
my mind began to think . . .
Who is it creeping up to our doorstep?
Who's getting our lovely orange
for their breakfast?

Someone on their way to work?
Someone walking a dog?
Someone who nips out and collects it
and nips back in again

and then shares it out round the family?

So I made a plan.

On Friday
I got up
same time as the milkman,
picked up the orange carton
took it indoors
emptied the orange out into a jug
poured in some orange squash
up to about five centimetres from the top
and then I took some
hot Jamaica sauce we've got.
And I don't know whether you know
what that's like
but if you just put a little speck of it
on your tongue
it feels as if someone's put a match
in your mouth.
I love it. I put it on my rice.
So I took this stuff
and I shook in half a bottle-load of it.
shuk shuk shuk shuk
yeah
shuk shuk shuk shuk
yeah.
Then I sealed up the carton

and put it back on our doorstep
in exactly the same place
and then I went back to bed.
Now I had wanted to stay awake
but I dozed off by mistake.
Anyway
when I got up
I went straight to the front door
opened it and
hohoho
there was one pint of milk
and NO orange.
I was so pleased.

And then I thought –
I made up a little scene in my mind.
I thought,
Maybe,
my orange thief *is*
someone who nips out
nicks the orange,
nips back in
and shares it out with the family.
So this morning,
this person did just that.
Gets back indoors,
opens up the orange
everyone sitting round the breakfast table

pours out a glass for everyone
lifts up the glass
and goes,
'Here's best wishes to those lovely people
at number 11
who give us our fresh orange.'
Raises it to the lips,
gulps,
and
phoooooor
It feels like someone's
jammed a banger in his mouth.

His mouth's on fire
And he goes dancing round the house
for the next hour,
stuffs his head under the tap
fills his mouth with water,
goes off dancing round the house again
he can't get rid of it.

Maybe that's what happened.
Maybe it didn't.
It could have been a woman
it could have been a kid.
All I know is
we haven't lost any more orange
since.

Hohohoho.

GYMNASTICS

When my mum and dad went out
we moved the chair to the end of the settee
and then we used to take it in turns
to do dive-bombs
off the chair
on to the settee.

Standby
wheeeeeeee
kerflump.
Great.

Jump down on to the floor
back on to the chair
standby for dive-bomb
wheeeeeeee
kerflump
wow did you see that one?

Then we put another chair
on the other end of the settee
and rammed the table up close to that chair.

Then you could dive-bomb
off the chair on to the settee
wheeeeeeee
kerflump
climb on to the chair at the other end of the settee
and then up on to the table
leap off the table
like a RED DEVIL
yahooooo
BAMM on to the floor.

Then we piled up all the cushions
in the corner
so you could go tunnelling
along the wall, round the corner

back to the chair next to the settee
jugga jugga jugga jugga
and banging your feet
on the floorboards
thudda thudda thudda thudda

Great.

I asked Harrybo, Tony Sanders,
Lizzie, Grey and Hendy over
and all seven of us went round

Great.

Next day,
we all met up
and it was Lizzie who said
after we've dive-bombed the settee
we could trampoline for a bit
bouncy bouncy bouncy bouncy
and then if we pulled the flaps
out of the table
we could do marching on the table
clomp clomp clomp clomp.

Great, I said
come over.

Yeah we'll come over
for gymnastics at Rosie's place.

So,
that night,
we dashed out of school
into our front room
moved the furniture round
and away we went.
Standby for dive-bomb
wheeeeeeee
kerflump on to the settee
trampoline
bouncy bouncy bouncy bouncy
up on to chair number two
up on to the table
march
clomp clomp clomp clomp

RED DEVIL
yahooooooo
BAMM on to the floor
jugga jugga jugga jugga jugga
under the cushions
thudda thudda thudda thudda
and back to chair number one
all seven of us
great

screaming our heads off
round and round
our gymnastics course.

The doorbell rang.

Right in the middle of our session.
The doorbell.

I went and answered the door.
It was the man from downstairs.
He looked at me for a long time
and then he started to speak.

'Is your father in?'

'No,' I said
'Tell him I want a word with him
when he comes in, will you?' he said.

'Yes,' I said.

He went on looking at me.
I could hear him breathing
and his eyes were getting big
his mouth was tightening up
then he shouted:
'MY LIGHT FITTING HAS JUST FALLEN OUT
OF MY CEILING!!!!
WHAT'S GOING ON?
I'VE NEVER HEARD ANYTHING LIKE IT.
WHAT HAVE YOU GOT IN THERE?
A WHOLE HERD OF ELEPHANTS?
MY LIGHT FITTING HAS JUST FALLEN OUT
OF MY CEILING.'

Then all quiet he said,
'I shall tell your mother and father
about this.
Don't you worry, sonny.
You'll see.'

He went indoors.

I dashed back into
the front room –
they were lying about all over the floor
panting and giggling.

'That was the man from downstairs.
He says we've bust his light or something.'
'Blimey,' one of them said.
'You're in trouble.'
'Yeah, Rosie's in trouble,' they said.
And they all got up off the floor
and dashed out of the house.

You can bet they didn't hang about
or anything.

PEBBLE

I know a man who's got a pebble.

He found it and he sucked it
during the war.
He found it and he sucked it
when they ran out of water.
He found it and he sucked it
when they were dying for a drink.
And he sucked it and he sucked it
for days and days and days.

I know a man who's got a pebble
and he keeps it in his drawer.

It's small and brown – nothing much to
look at
but I think of the things he thinks
when he sees it:

how he found it
how he sucked it
how he nearly died for water to drink.

A small brown pebble
tucked under his tongue
and he keeps it in his drawer
to look at now and then.

UNFAIR

When we went over the park
Sunday mornings
to play football
we picked up sides.

Lizzie was our striker
because she had the best shot.

When the teachers
chose the school team
Marshy was our striker.

Lizzie wasn't allowed to play,
they said.

So she watched us lose, instead . . .

LOSING THINGS

I HATE LOSING THINGS
so I think,
'What if
there is a place somewhere
where everything you ever lost
goes?'

Somehow or another
all those things you ever lost
found their way there –
to this place?

Maybe there's a huge hall somewhere
with hundreds and hundreds of doors
and one of the doors
has got your name on it.

I see myself
going to this huge hall one day.

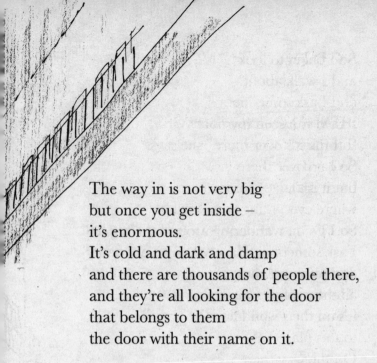

The way in is not very big
but once you get inside –
it's enormous.
It's cold and dark and damp
and there are thousands of people there,
and they're all looking for the door
that belongs to them
the door with their name on it.

Everyone is asking everyone else:
'Have you seen my door?'
'What's your name?'
And people are saying things like –
'I think I saw it over there.'
or,
'Don't bother me, I'm looking for mine.'

So I begin to look
and I walk about
and I ask someone:
'Have you seen my door?'
'I think it's over there,' she says.
So I go over there –
but it isn't.

So I go on wandering around the big hall.
I ask someone: 'Have you seen my door?'
and someone says,
'Up the spiral stair –
it's on the second floor.'

On the way there
someone stops me and says,
'Have you seen my door?'
and I say, 'No, I haven't.'
I climb up the spiral stair
on to the second floor
but my door isn't there either.

So I go on wandering around the big hall

And someone comes up to me and says,
'Have you seen my door?'
'Have you seen mine?' I say.
'It's at the end by the steel doors,'

and it is.

It's my door.
It's got my name on it.

I knock on the door.
'Who's there?'
'Me.'
'We were expecting you.'

The bolts draw back,
the door opens
and two old people let me in
and shut the door behind me.

'It's all here,' one of them says.
'It's all here,' the other one says.

And they're right.

There's my penknife from Switzerland,
I lost when I was twelve
the old watch I lost in my car accident
my blue anorak with the hood
that I left on a railway station in Paris
my round gold sunglasses
that I once wore in a play
to make me look blind
the football
that was a birthday present
that I lost on the same day I got it
over a wall in the burnt out church.

They're all there.

A black, white and green towel,
a Moroccan-leather wallet.

'They're all here,' says one of the old people.
'They're all here,' says the other.

'Have you got a bag to take them away in?'
says one.

'Here's a bag to take them away in,' says the other.
So I fill up the bag
with all the things that I've ever lost
until all the shelves are empty.

'Come back and see us any time,' says one.
'Come back and see us,' says the other.
'You know where we are now, don't you?' says one.
'You know where we are,' says the other.

'But you're taking my name off the door,' I say.
'Why are you taking my name off the door?'
'Because you know where we are now, don't you?'
     says one.
'You know where we are,' says the other.

And they shut the door.
I hear the locks and bolts on the door

and I walk away into the crowd
in the huge hall,
and everyone is still walking round
asking everyone else,
'Do you know where my door is?'

A tall man with a steering wheel in his hand
says to me,
'You seen my door, have you?'
'No,' I say. 'No.'
'No, I don't expect you have,' he says.

I look round to see if I can remember
where my door was.
And it's out of sight.
Too many people are in the way.
So I say to myself,
'One day,
I'll try and find my way back there,'
but something tells me,
some little voice in my head says,
'I bet you'll never ever find that door again.
You've had the only chance
you'll ever have.'

So I make my way
out of that huge dark hall
with the thousands and thousands of doors
and the thousands and thousands of people

and I hurry home with my bag
and I get back to my room
and I spread out on the floor
all those things that I had lost
and I've now got back again,

and that makes me very happy.

CHRISTMAS DINNER

We were all sitting round the table.
There was roast turkey
there were roast potatoes
there were roast parsnips
there were broccoli tips
there was a dishful of crispy bacon off the turkey
there was wine, cider, beer, lemonade
and milk – for the youngsters.
Everything was set.

It was all on the table.
We were ready to begin.
Suddenly there was a terrible terrible scream.
Right next to the turkey was a worm.
A dirty little worm wriggling about like mad.
For a moment everyone looked at it.
Someone said very quietly, 'Oh dear.'
And everyone was thinking things like –
'How did it get there?'
'If that came out of the turkey,
I don't want any of it.'
or,
'I'm not eating any Christmas dinner. It could be full of
dirty little wriggly worms.'

Now – as it happens,
I don't mind wriggly worms.
There was plenty of room for it
at the table.
It was just that . . . that . . .
no one had asked it to come over
for Christmas dinner.

So I said,
'I don't think it came out of the turkey. I think –
It came off the bottom of the milk bottle.'
And I picked up the worm,

and put it out the door to spend Christmas day
in a lovely patch of wet mud.
Much nicer place to be –
for a worm.

I'M NOT GOING PLACES WITH THEM AGAIN

When we went to Chessington Zoo
with the club
we all went in
and the leader said,
'Right, listen, everyone,
listen, everyone,
everyone listen.
You can all go off where you like
for the next two hours
and we'll all meet up here
at 4 o'clock.
At 4 o'clock,
OK?'

Then we all went off
where we liked.

I saw the lions
and the seals
and the parrots

and the giraffes
and the crocodiles.
I ate my cheese and pickle sandwiches
a packet of crisps
and drank some of my fizzy orange
and ate a chocolate swiss roll.

Then I asked someone the time
and she said, '4 o'clock,'
so I went back to where we had to meet.

When I got there
everyone started shouting at me.

'Where have you been?
Where do you think you've been?
We've been looking for you for hours
we couldn't find you anywhere

we've scarcely had a chance to see
any of the animals
where have you been?'
I looked at them
and I said,
'I've been walking round the zoo.
I'm on time, aren't I?'

So then they started shouting at me again.

'You weren't supposed
to wander off on your own, were you?
You were supposed to be in your
group.
Everyone else was in their
groups.
You weren't, were you?'

'No.'

'Well, we've got to go now.
Just think, you've spoiled
everyone's afternoon, now.'

I listened to all that
but I wasn't sorry.
They said,
'You can all go off now.'
They didn't say anything about
groups.
What groups?
I'm not going places with them again.

SHUT YOUR MOUTH WHEN YOU'RE EATING

Shut your mouth when you're eating.

> I am, Dad.

MOUTH!

> It *is* shut.

I can see it isn't. I can *hear* it isn't.

> What about *his* mouth? You can see
> *everything* in his mouth.

He's only two. He doesn't know any better.

> You can see all his peas and tomato sauce.

That's none of your business.

(2 MINUTES GO BY)

> Dad.

Yes.

> Your mouth's open. Shut your mouth
> when you're eating.

It is shut, thank you very much.

> I can see it isn't, Dad. I can see all the food
> in there.

157

Look that's my business, OK?
Peas, gravy, spuds, everything.
Look, you don't want to grow up to be as horrible
as your father
do you? Answer that, smartyboots.

NOTHING MUCH

'What did you do on Friday?'
'Nothing much –
I like doing nothing quite often –
like putting on old hats
or drawing forests along the edges
of the newspapers we keep under the sink.
How about you?'

'I showed my mum and dad
what I had made in school that week.
It was a lorry
that works on elastic bands
and my dad said:
"What did you make that thing for?"
I bet he played with it when I went to bed.'

EDDIE AND THE SHREDDIES

The other day Eddie
was eating his Shreddies –
you know what Shreddies are:
those little bits of cardboard
you have for breakfast.

Sometimes he forgets where his mouth is
and he stuffs a Shreddie in his ear.
Doesn't worry him.
He takes it out and puts it in his mouth.

Anyway,
I left my hairbrush on the table
while he was eating his Shreddies
and I went out of the room.

While I was out
Eddie found somewhere else
to put his Shreddies.
On my hairbrush.

When I came back in
I picked up my hairbrush
and brushed my hair . . .

Yuk.

Shreddies in my hair.
I looked at Eddie,
Eddie's looking at me.
Big grin on his face.

I knew he had done it.
Last week he put pepper in the raisins.

MY MAGIC BOX

When Aladdin rubbed the lamp
a genie came to him and said,
'I am at your service.
I will do whatever you wish.'

I wanted to have a genie.
My genie,
but no matter how many old lamps
I rubbed,
no genie came to me.

But –
one morning I was daydreaming.
The window was open.
'I want to fly out of the window,' I said.
'I want to fly,' I said.
'I want to fly,'
and
kerchung!
into my hand came a shiny black box
like a cassette recorder

with silver levers and buttons and switches
and little flaps that clipped down
with silver studs.
One of the flaps said, FLY,
so I undid the studs

lifted the flap
and there was a button underneath it.
So I pressed it
and next thing I knew
I was flying.
I was flying with my black box
tucked underneath my arm.

I flew up off my bed
and out through the window
flying, really flying,
and I didn't come down again.

I went
weeeeeeeeeeeeeeeeeeeeeeeee
till I heard,
'He's in one of his dreams,'
and suddenly I wasn't flying.
I didn't have my box.
I was just standing in the middle of the room.
After that time
that first time

I found all kinds of ways
to get my black box with the silver switches
and buttons.

Sometimes I just wished

for the box to come to me
and we went places together.

Other times
I wished for something
and without even waiting for me to wish for it
my box came and helped me.

You see,
I love hot beaches
I love to walk on a hot beach
the sun hot on my back
the sea cool under my feet
and I grow thirsty
as I walk.
The sun hot
the sea cool
my mouth begins to dry out
so I wish for something
to wet those dry lips
something icy
something to lick
a lolly to lick
so with the sun hot on my back
the sea wet on my feet

I want
a lolly cold on my lips,
and
kerchung!

There's my black box
silver switches, buttons, levers
and this time
when I see a flap
the flap says, 'Lolly.'
I lift the flap
I press the button
and the lolly comes into my hand
raspberry
raspberry split
so I can lick
and nibble

with the sun still hot on my back
and the sea still wet on my feet
and my box underneath my arm
then I hear
'Hey you, I asked you to get dressed
an hour ago'

and the sun goes
the sea goes
the lolly goes
the box goes

and I'm just
sitting in the middle of the floor
with a pair of trousers in my hands.

It was a good friend,
my box,
kept me out of trouble,
my box,
stayed with me when I was ill,
my box.

TODAY I ATE

Today I ate

2 ham sandwiches

4 strawberry cream wafers

a Pepsi

2 bubblegums

a Cornetto

3 Yorkies

2 chocolate biscuits

3 plain biscuits

a fizzy orange

a hamburger

a plate of chips

and a Pepsi.

At four o'clock I went to bed;

at four thirty I was sick.

I sicked up

a Pepsi

a plate of chips

a hamburger

a fizzy orange

3 plain biscuits

2 chocolate biscuits

3 Yorkies

a Cornetto

two bubblegums

a Pepsi

4 strawberry cream wafers

and 2 ham sandwiches.

Tomorrow I won't eat
2 ham sandwiches
4 strawberry cream wafers
a Pepsi
2 bubblegums
a Cornetto
3 Yorkies
2 chocolate biscuits
3 plain biscuits
a fizzy orange
a hamburger
a plate of chips
and a Pepsi.

The day after tomorrow
I may have a
Pepsi
I may have a
hamburger
I may have a Cornetto
but not just now thanks . . .

SNAILS

When my last tadpole died
and my one fish
the loach
disappeared into the middle
of the dark green tank
and never came out again;
when you couldn't see anything
in there any more
they all came
my brother
my mum
my dad
and looked at the tank and laughed:
'Why don't you clean it out?'
'Nothing can live in there.'
'Why do you keep it?'
I knew why.

My oldest and best snail
was in there
climbing up and down the sides
of the tank.
A big brown snail she was
and just recently
not long ago
I had seen some tiny, tiny snails
on the glass
each one smaller than a Rice Krispie.

They must have come out of the spawn
she laid.

But they didn't know what I was thinking.

'What have you got in there, then?'
'Even the pondweed's dead.'

'Snails.'

There was nothing they could say to that . . .
except laugh their heads off.

DRACULA MASK

Once there was a boy
who was never ever scared.

And he went to a joke shop
and bought a terrible mask.

It looked a bit like a skull
it looked a bit like a Dracula
it looked a bit like a Fiend
and it glowed in the dark.

Green.
It was horrible.

So the boy put the mask on
and ran about all over the place.
He ran up to the big boys next door
and went,
'Grrrrrrrrr
whoo-hoo whoo-hoo
sssssssssss . . .'

and they laughed.

So he went to the park
and there were some ducks

and so he went,
'Grrrrrrrrrrr
whoo-hoo whoo-hoo
sssssssss . . .'
and the ducks swam slowly round and round and round
looking for bits of bread.

So he went up to his dad
and went,
'Grrrrrrrrrrr
whoo-hoo whoo-hoo
sssssssss . . .'

and his dad looked at him and said,
'We should have brought some bread for the ducks.'

So he rushed up to
a big
woolly
mongrel
dog
and went,
'Grrrrrrrr
whoo-hoo whoo-hoo whoo-hoo
sssssssss . . .'

and the dog went,

'Wuff wuff wuff,'
very loudly
and rushed at that
green Dracula skull fiend
and tried to bite its head off.

And the green Dracula skull fiend ran
and the green Dracula skull fiend screamed,
it went,
'Daddy Daddy Daddy
help me help me help me.'

So,
it can be very very scary
trying to make
a big woolly mongrel dog
very very scared . . .

GUMDROPS

When Harrybo was really happy about something
when he was really pleased
he used to go,
'Goody goody gumdrops
save me when my bum pops.'

INDEX OF FIRST LINES

POETRY Pie

HOT OR TAKEAWAY POETRY

CATCH ME

WE'RE ALL LOVIN OUR POETRY PIE

ROGER McGOUGH

PUFFIN POETRY

'Roger McGough is a true original and more than one generation would be much the poorer without him' – *The Times Educational Supplement*

'Very silly, utterly crazy humour' – Jeremy Strong,
Guardian

'. . . A collection that works well on the page
and is a delight to read aloud' – *Guardian*

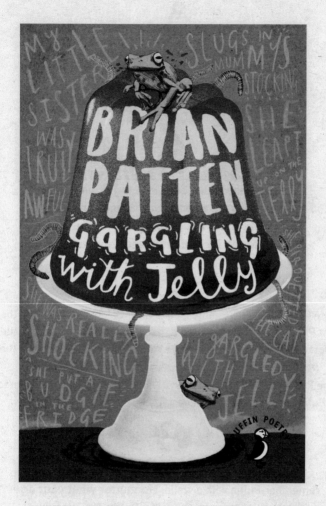

Full of Brian Patten's wonderful wit!

It all started with a Scarecrow

Puffin is over seventy years old.
Sounds ancient, doesn't it? But Puffin has never been
so lively. We're always on the lookout for the next big
idea, which is how it began all those years ago.

Penguin Books was a big idea from the mind of
a man called Allen Lane, who in 1935 invented
the quality paperback and changed the world.
**And from great Penguins, great Puffins grew,
changing the face of children's books forever.**

The first four Puffin Picture Books were hatched in 1940 and the
first Puffin story book featured a man with broomstick arms called
Worzel Gummidge. In 1967 Kaye Webb, Puffin Editor, started the
Puffin Club, promising to **'make children into readers'**.
She kept that promise and over 200,000 children became devoted
Puffineers through their quarterly instalments of *Puffin Post*.

Many years from now, we hope you'll look back and
remember Puffin with a smile. **No matter what your age
or what you're into, there's a Puffin for everyone.**
The possibilities are endless, but one thing is for sure:
whether it's a picture book or a paperback, a sticker book
or a hardback, **if it's got that little Puffin
on it – it's bound to be good.**

www.puffinbooks.com